LIGHT CLASSICAL PIECES FOR
ACCORDION

ARRANGED BY GARY MEISNER

T0085326

ISBN 978-1-4234-9928-2

HAL•LEONARD®
CORPORATION
7777 W. BLUEMOUND RD. P.O. BOX 13819 MILWAUKEE, WI 53213

In Australia Contact:
Hal Leonard Australia Pty. Ltd.
4 Lentara Court
Cheltenham, Victoria, 3192 Australia
Email: ausadmin@halleonard.com.au

Visit Hal Leonard Online at
www.halleonard.com

BARCAROLLE
from THE TALES OF HOFFMANN (LES CONTES D'HOFFMANN)

By JACQUES OFFENBACH

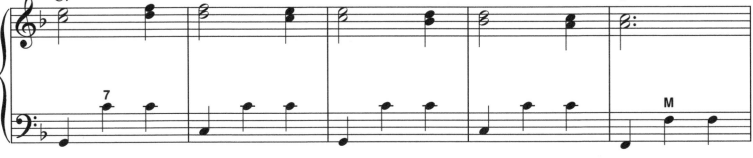

3

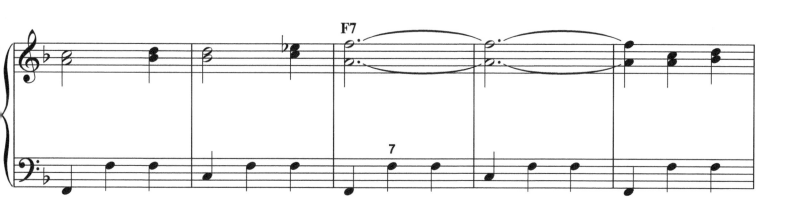

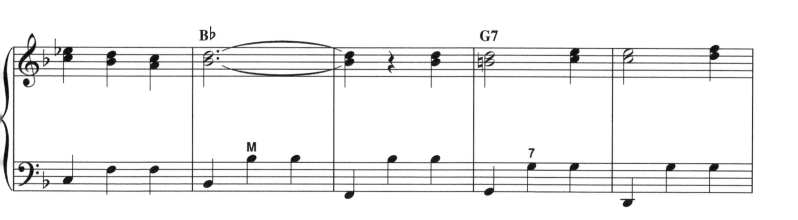

4

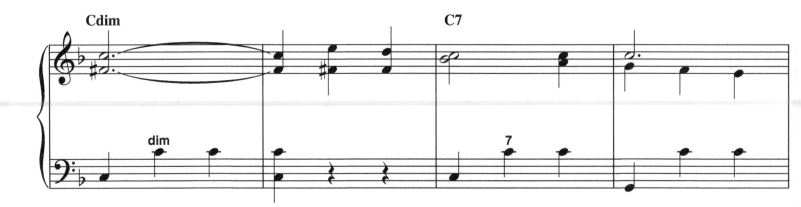

D.C. al Coda
(with repeat)

CODA

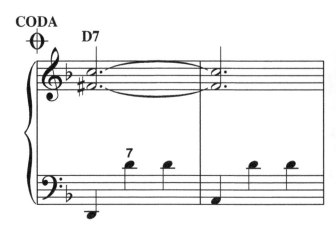

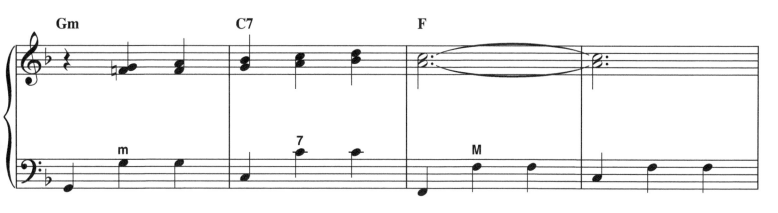

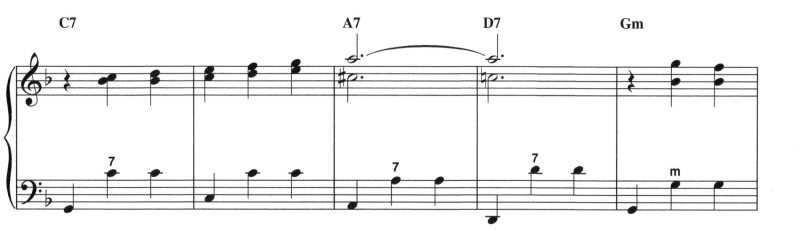

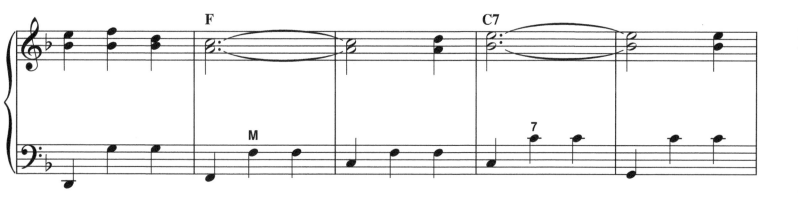

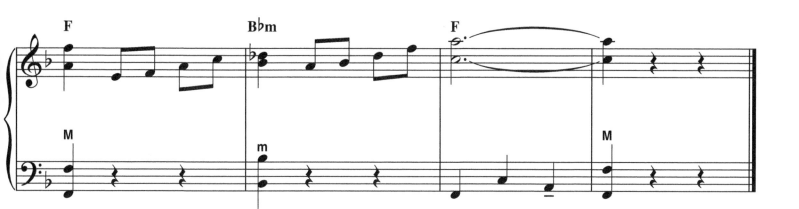

FUNERAL MARCH OF A MARIONETTE

By CHARLES GOUNOD

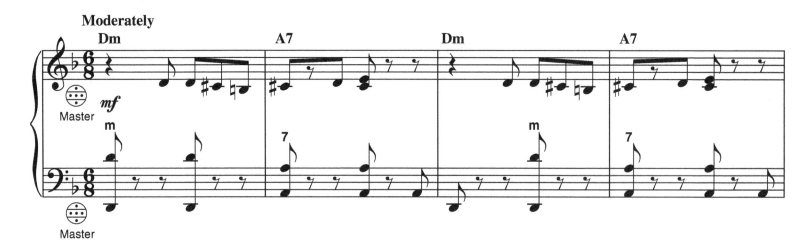

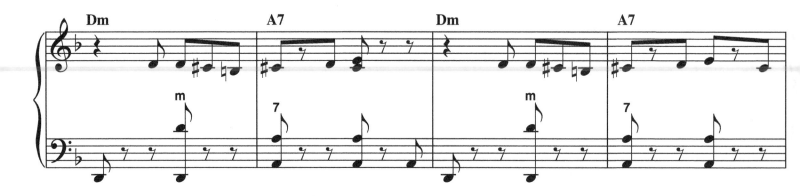

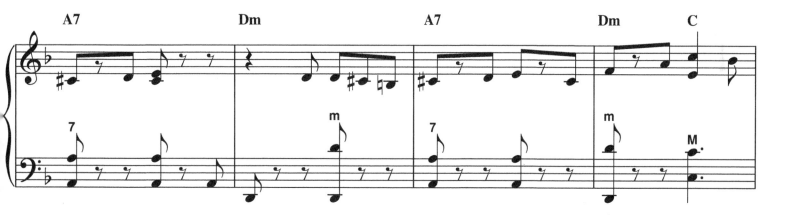

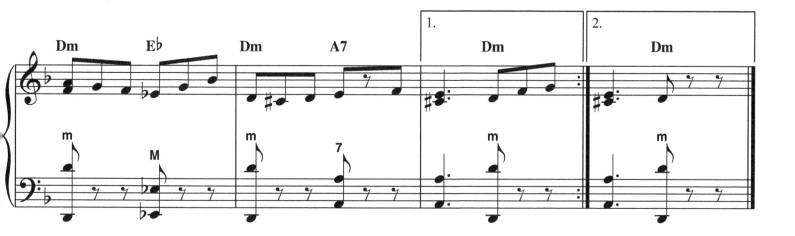

FÜR ELISE

By LUDWIG VAN BEETHOVEN

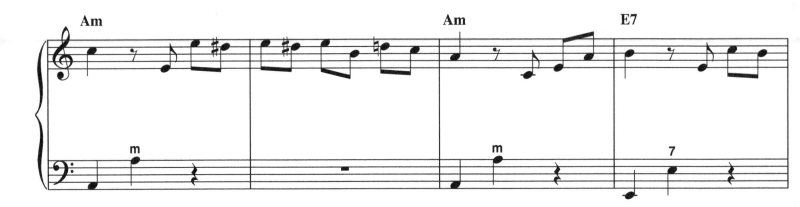

HUMORESQUE

By ANTONIN DVOŘÁK

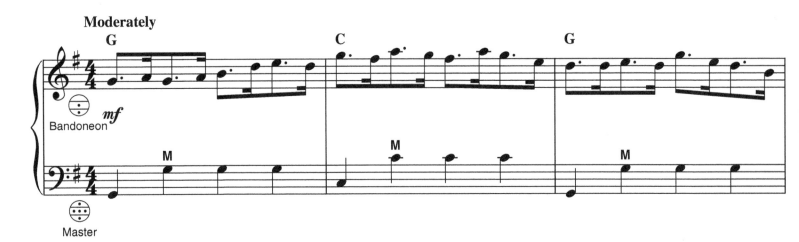

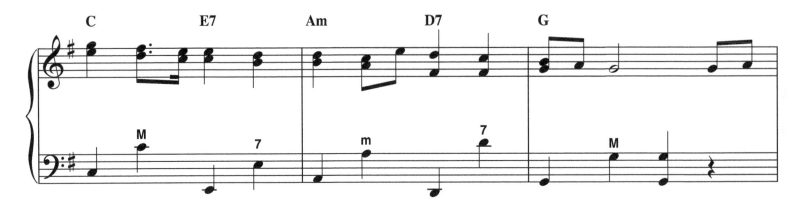

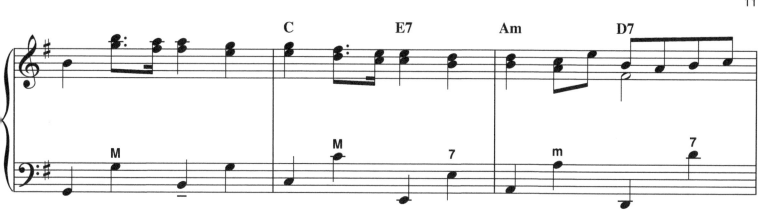

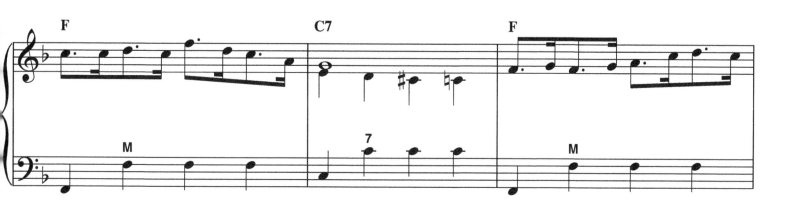

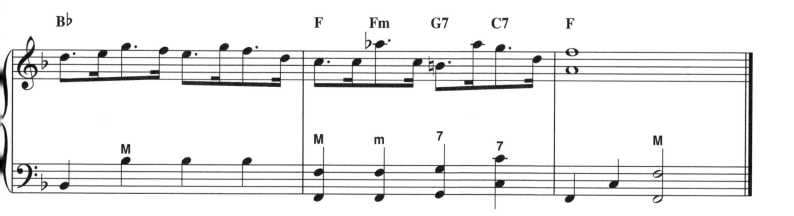

INDIAN SUMMER

Words and Music by
VICTOR HERBERT

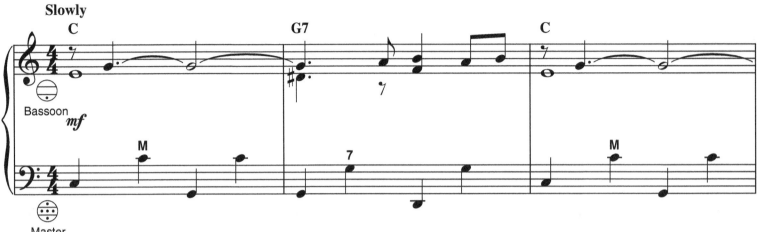

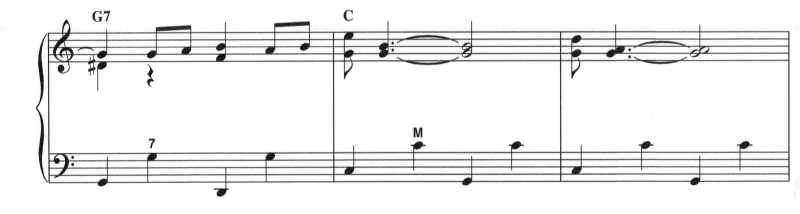

LA CINQUANTAINE
(The Golden Wedding)

By J. GABRIEL-MARIE

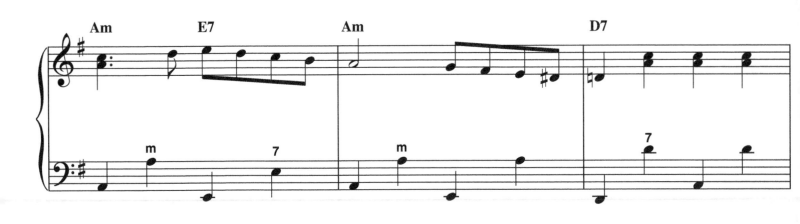

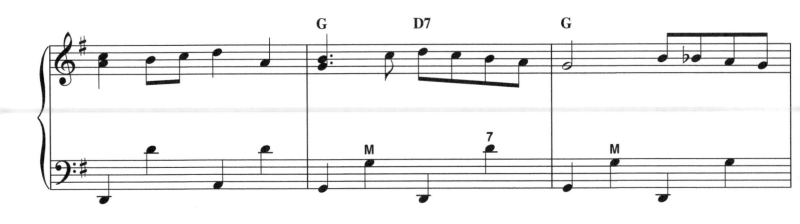

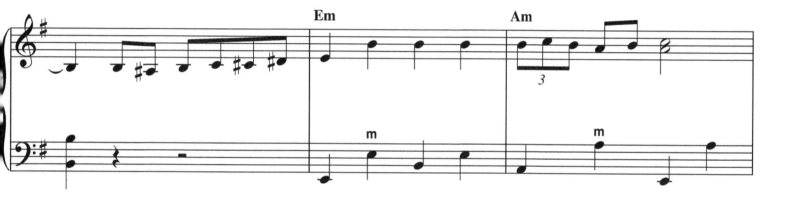

JESU, JOY OF MAN'S DESIRING

By JOHANN SEBASTIAN BACH

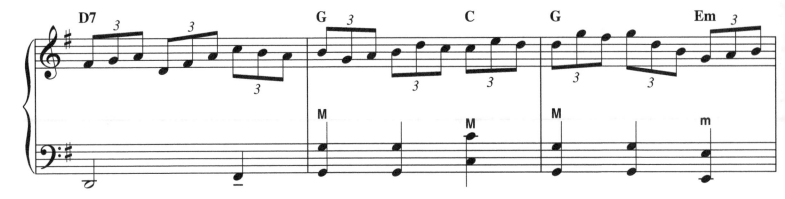

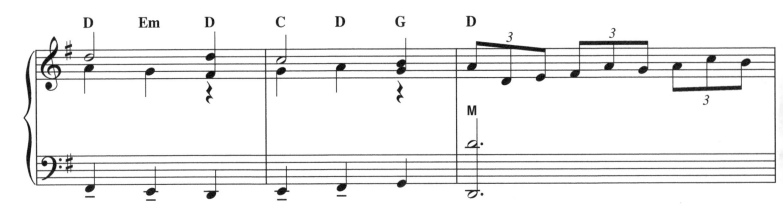

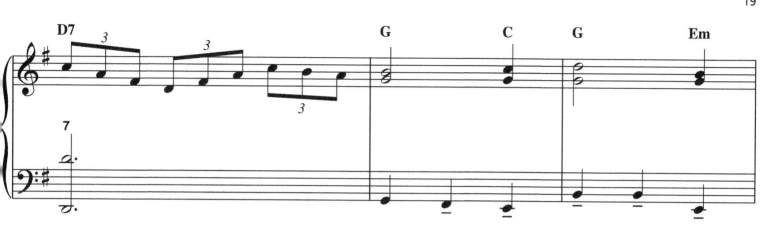

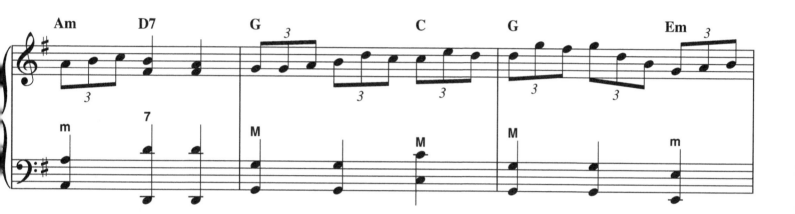

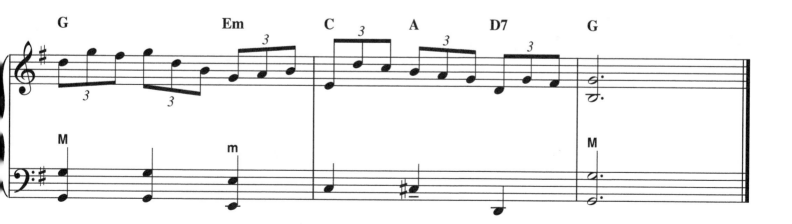

JULIET'S WALTZ SONG

By CHARLES GOUNOD

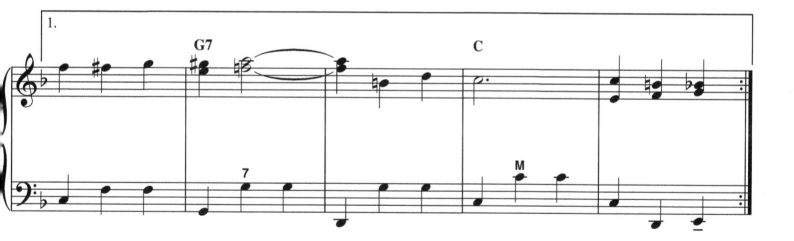

LA DONNA È MOBILE

from RIGOLETTO

By GIUSEPPE VERDI

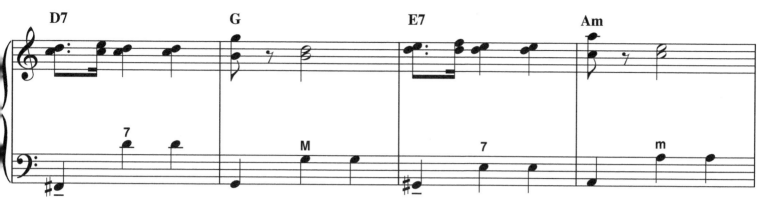

MINUET IN G MAJOR

By LUDWIG VAN BEETHOVEN

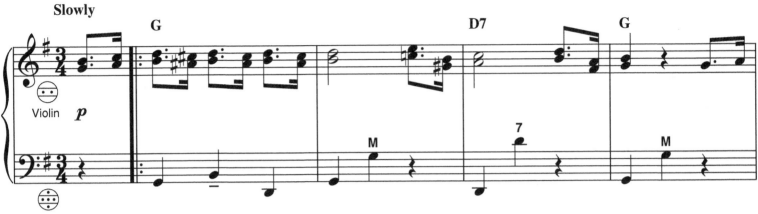

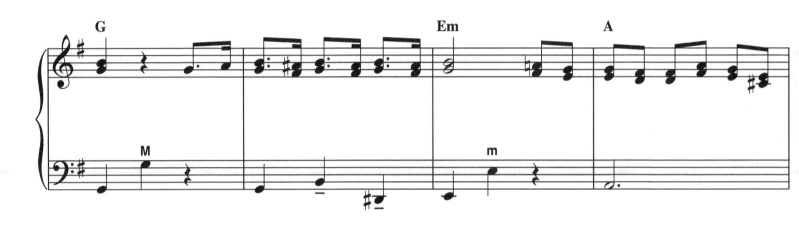

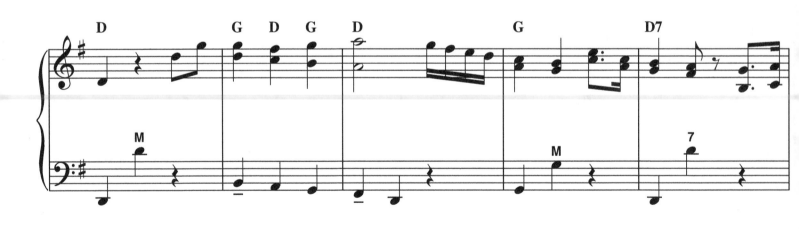

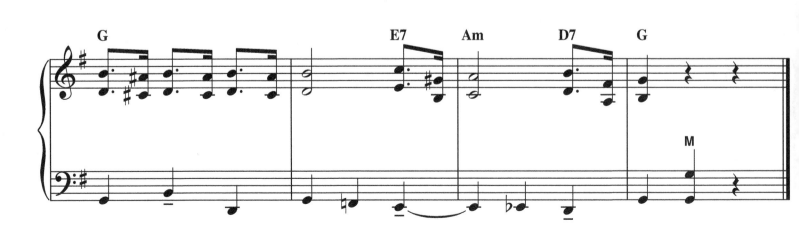

POMP AND CIRCUMSTANCE

Words by ARTHUR BENSON
Music by EDWARD ELGAR

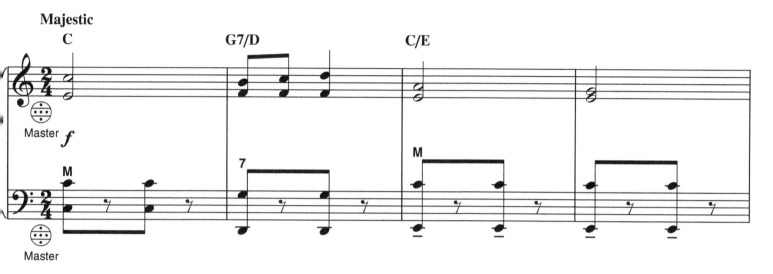

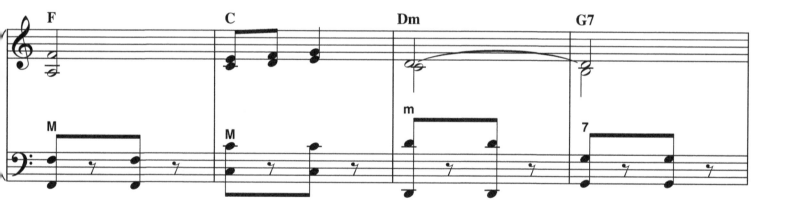

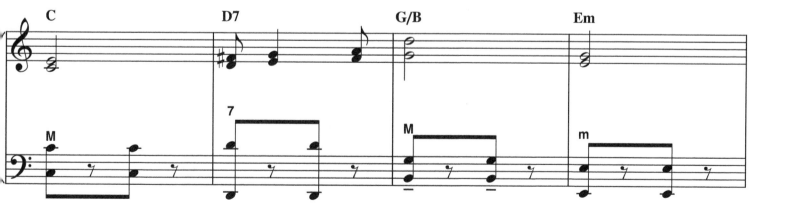

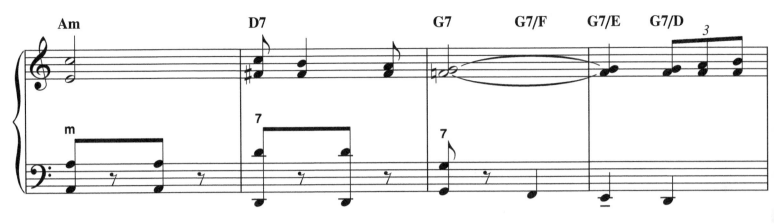

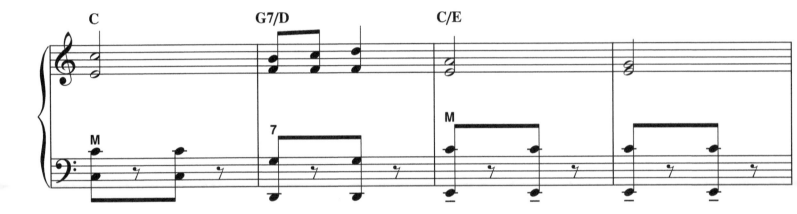

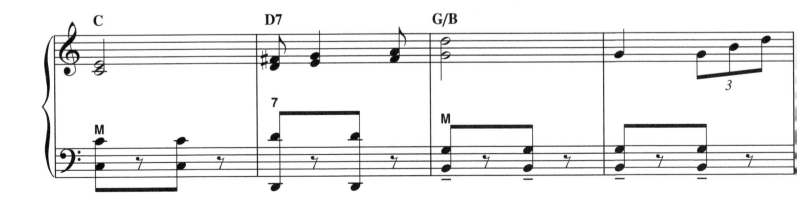

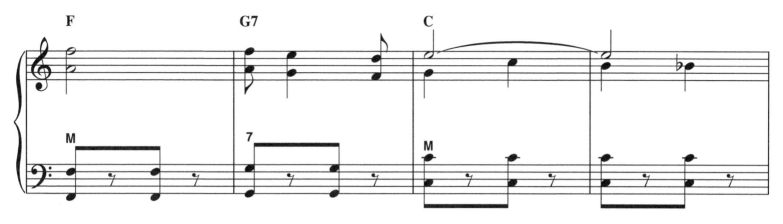

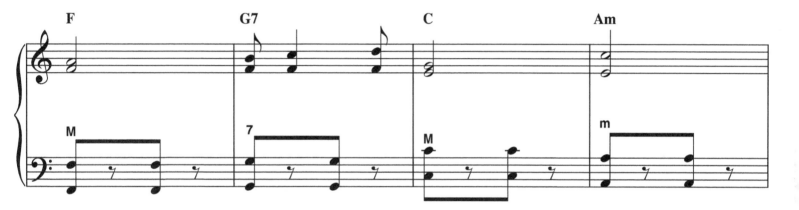

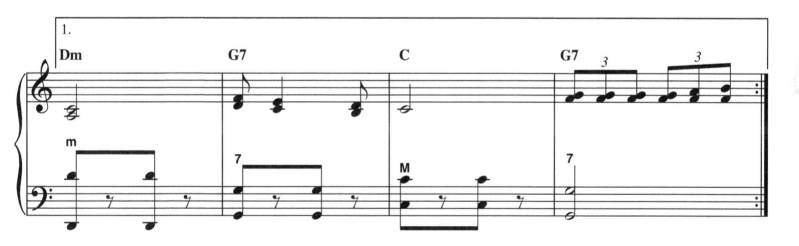

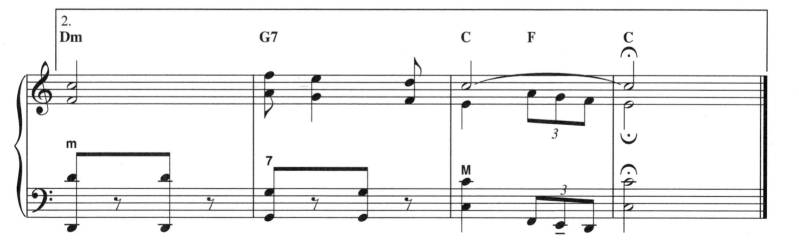

POLOVTSIAN DANCE THEME

By ALEXANDER BORODIN

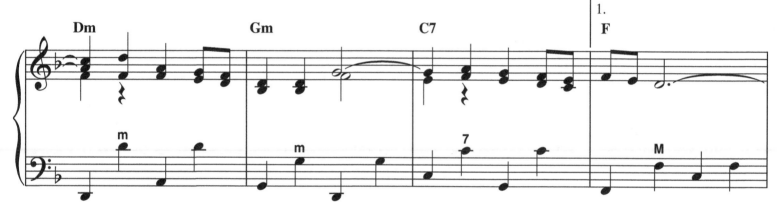

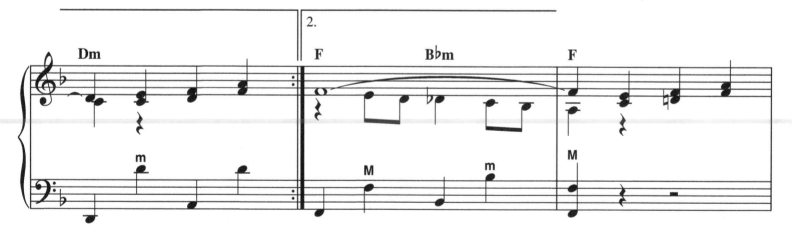

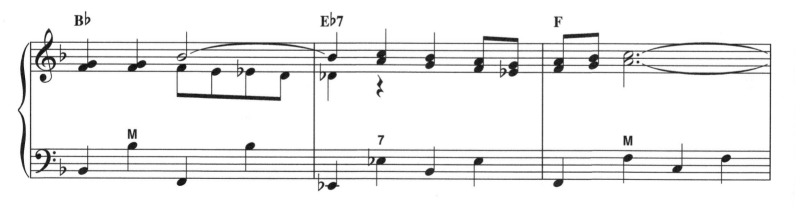

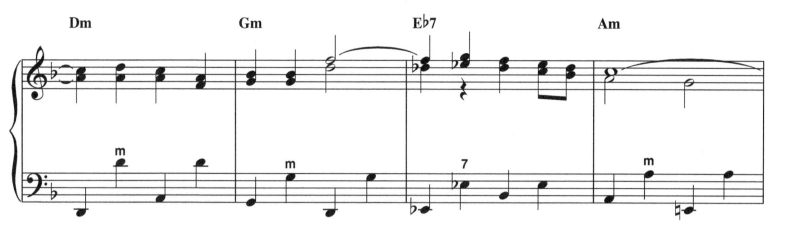

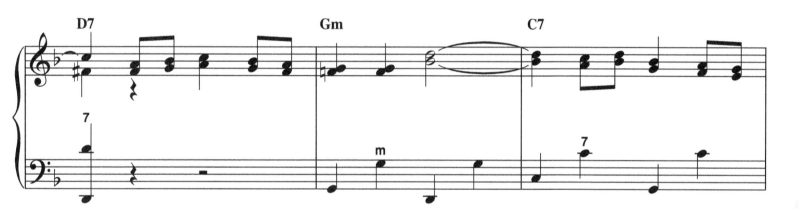

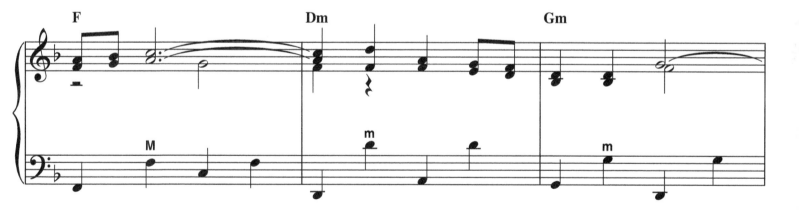

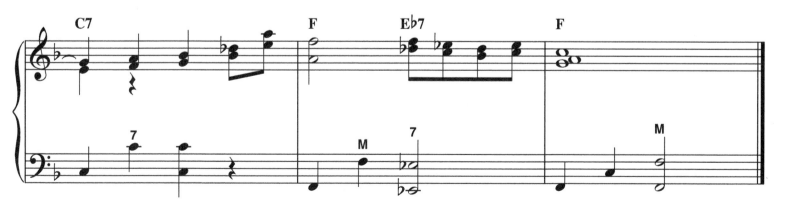

ROMANCE

By A. RUBINSTEIN

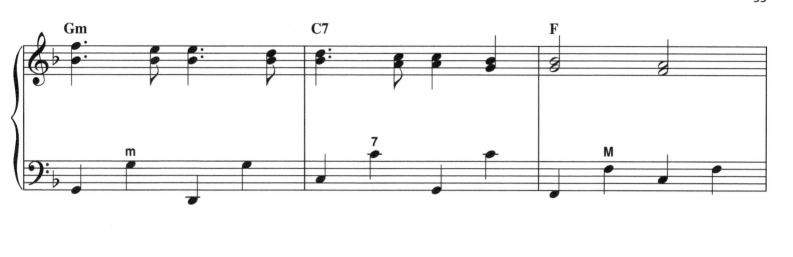

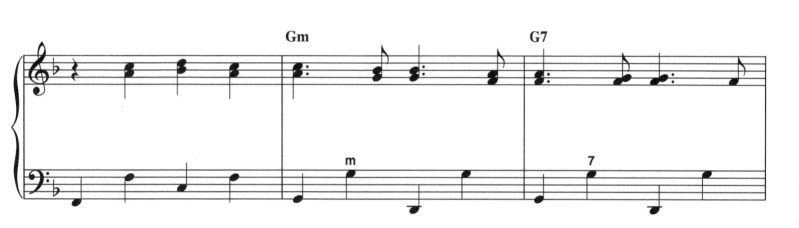

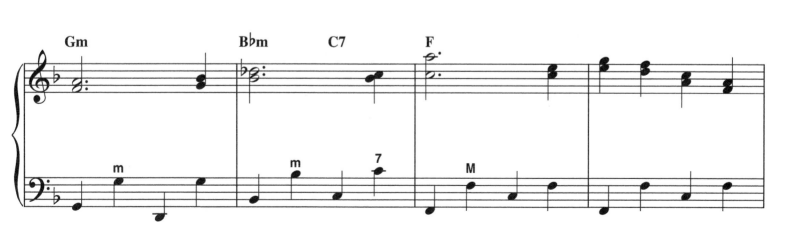

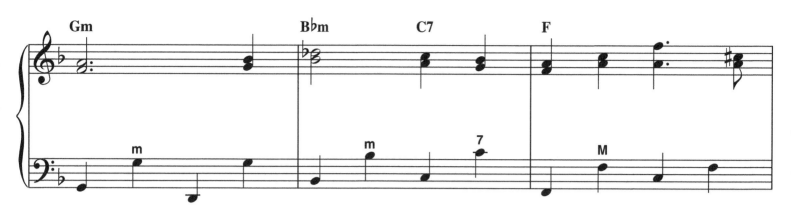

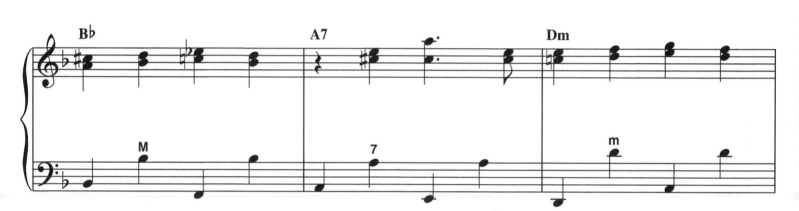

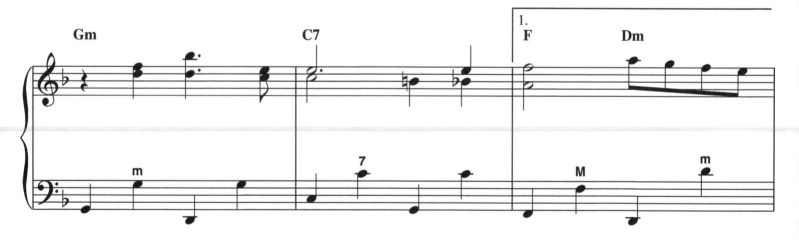

SERENADE

By RICCARDO DRIGO

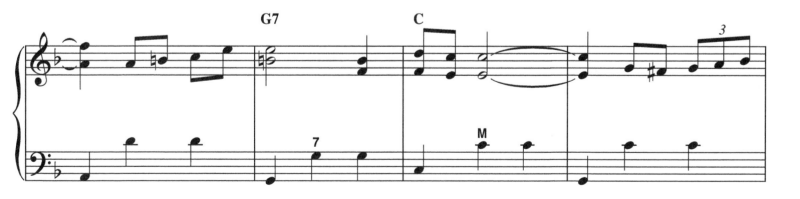

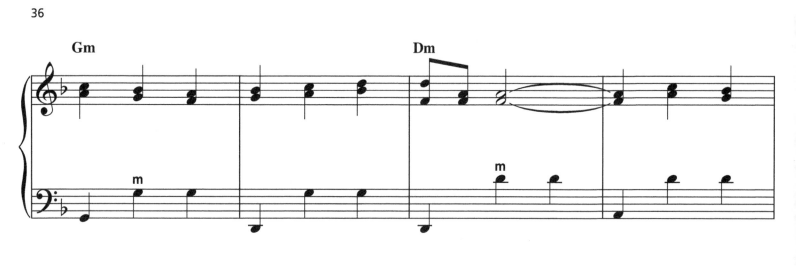

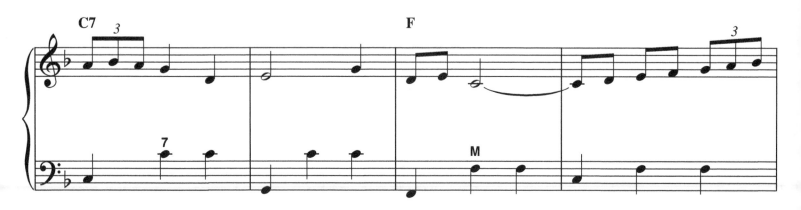

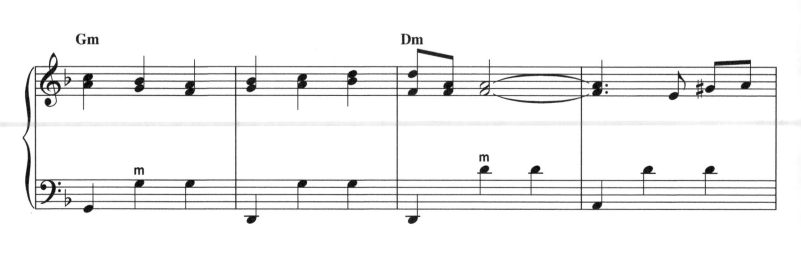

THE SLEEPING BEAUTY WALTZ

By PYOTR IL'YICH TCHAIKOVSKY

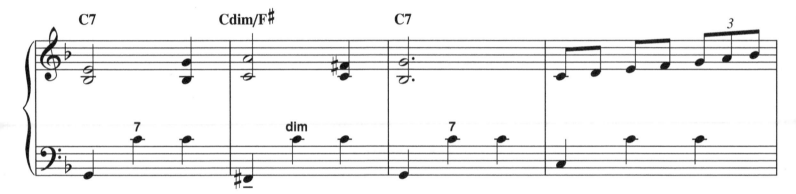

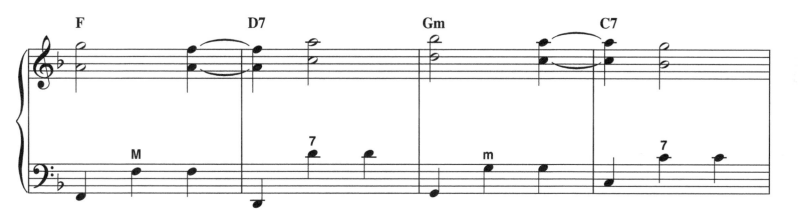

THEME FROM SWAN LAKE

By PYOTR IL'YICH TCHAIKOVSKY

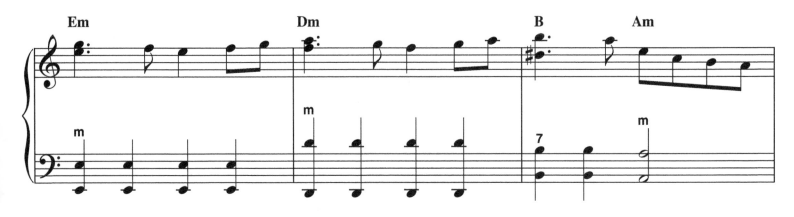

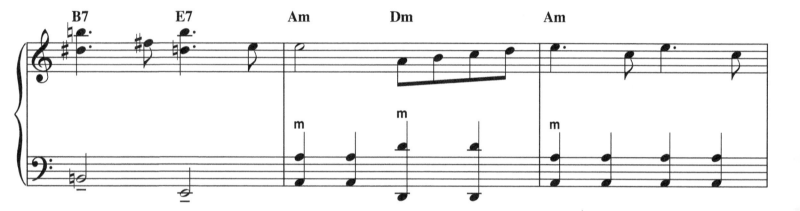

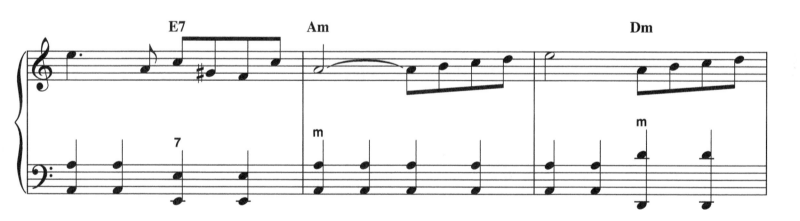

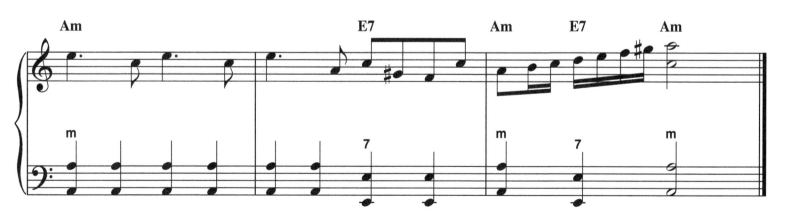

TALES FROM THE VIENNA WOODS

By JOHANN STRAUSS, JR.

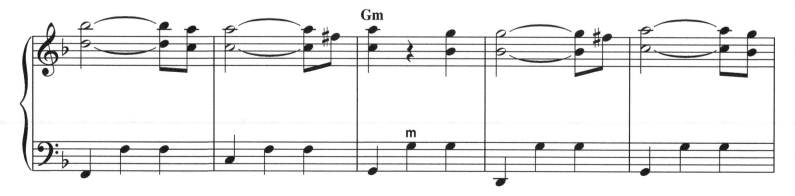

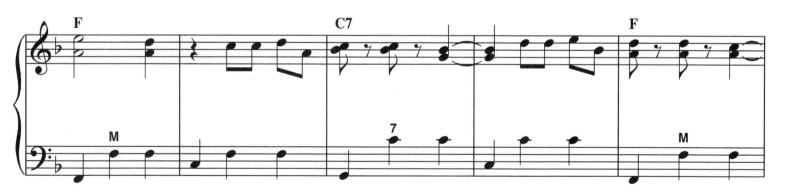

44

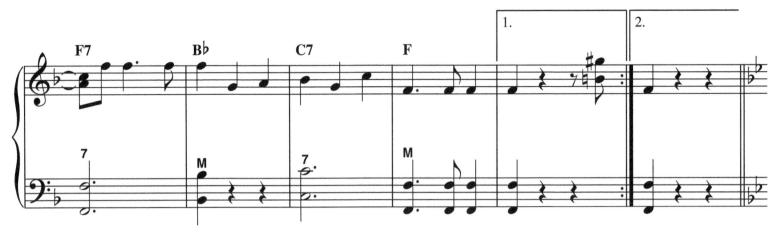

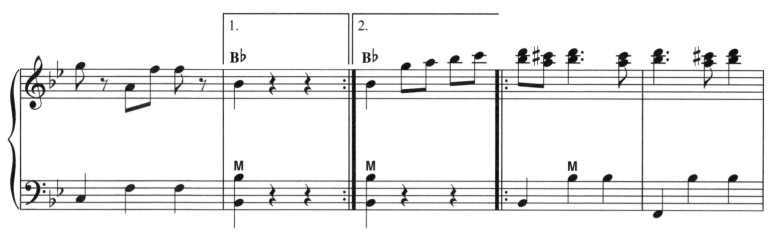

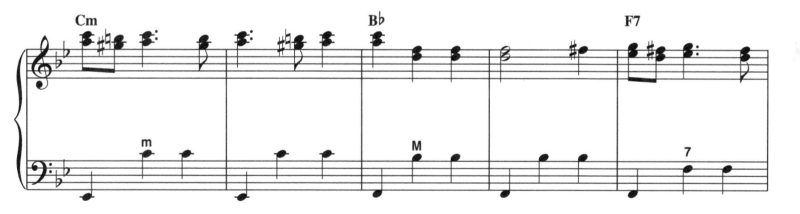

TO A WILD ROSE
from WOODLAND SKETCHES

By EDWARD MacDOWELL

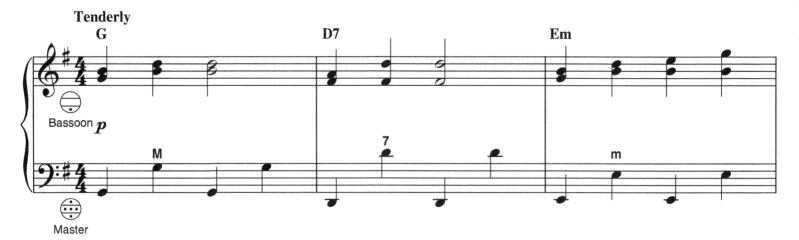

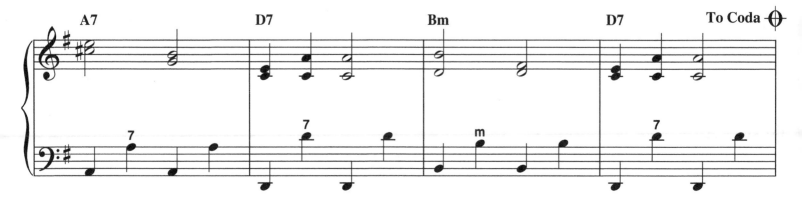

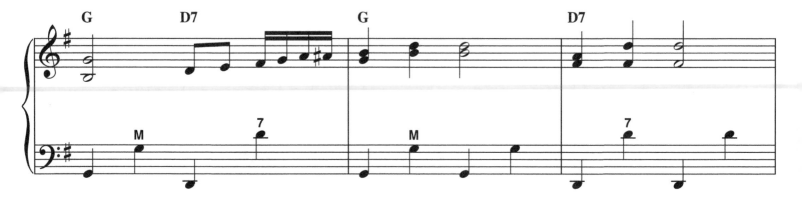

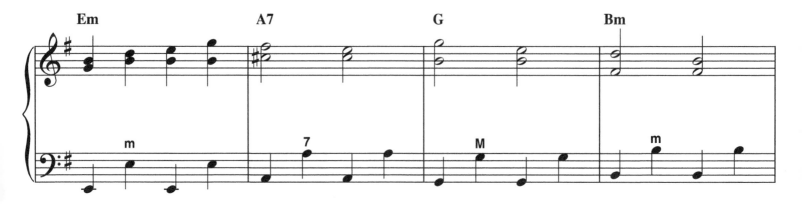

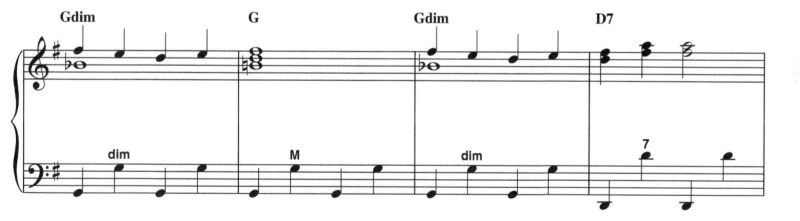

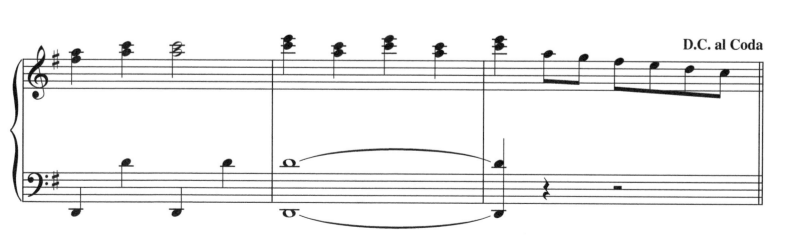

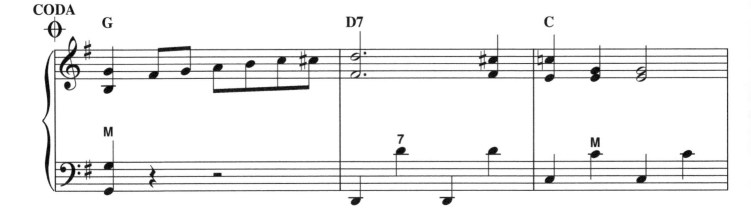

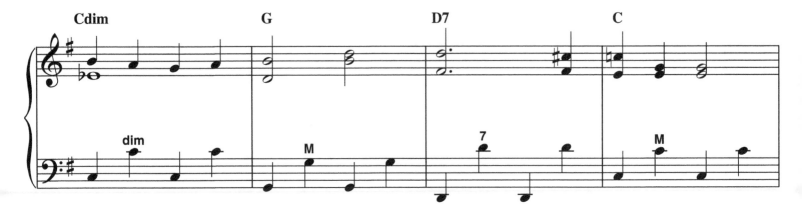

TRUMPET VOLUNTARY

By JEREMIAH CLARKE

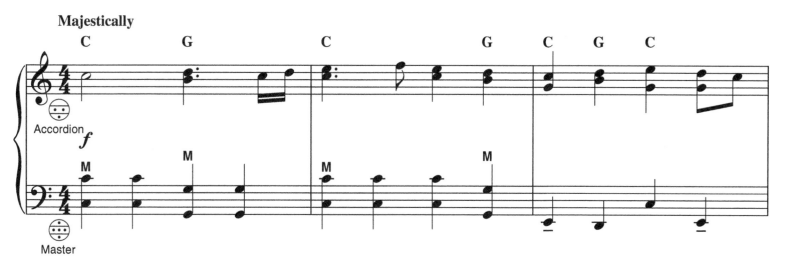

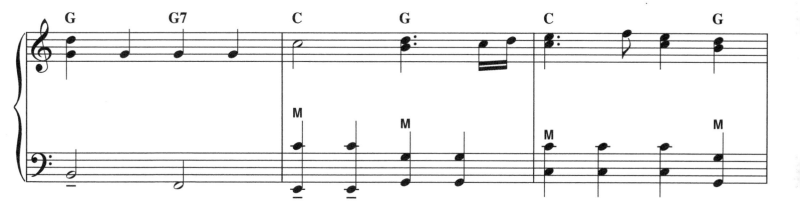

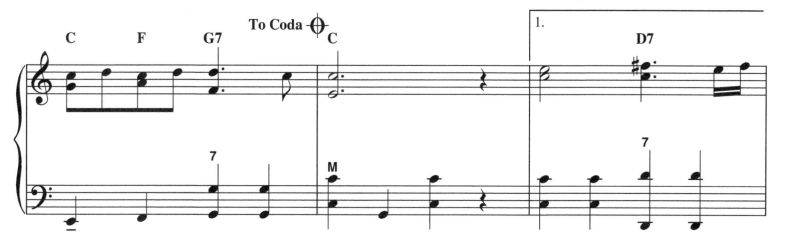

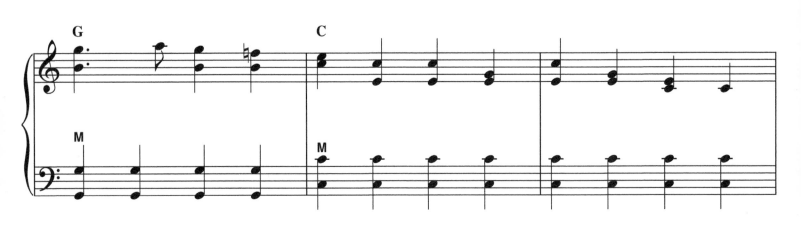

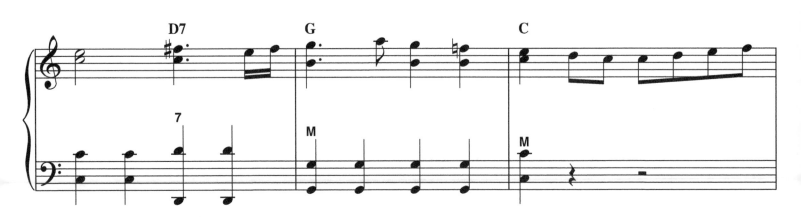

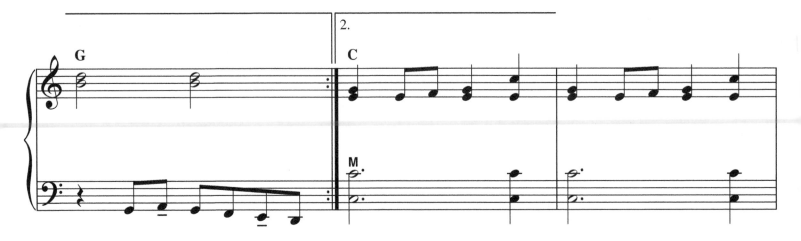

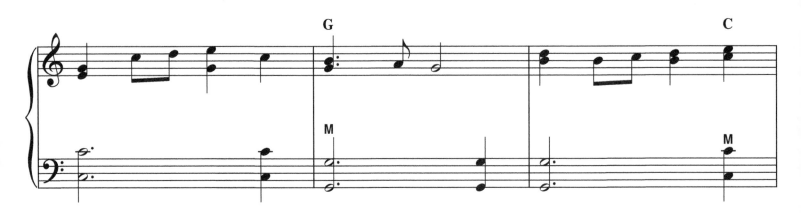

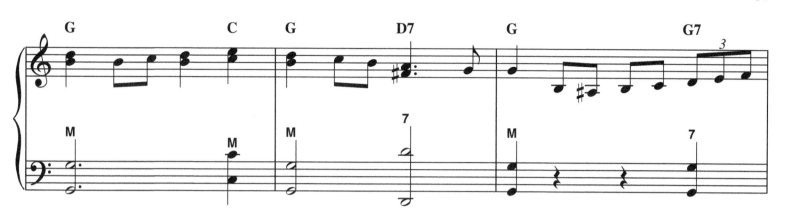

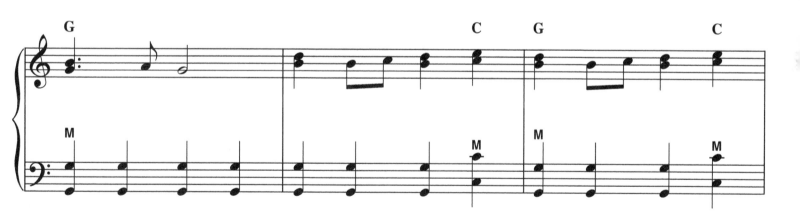

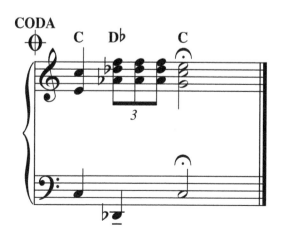

TRUMPET TUNE

By HENRY PURCELL

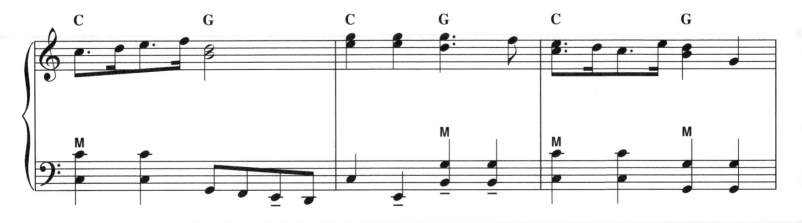

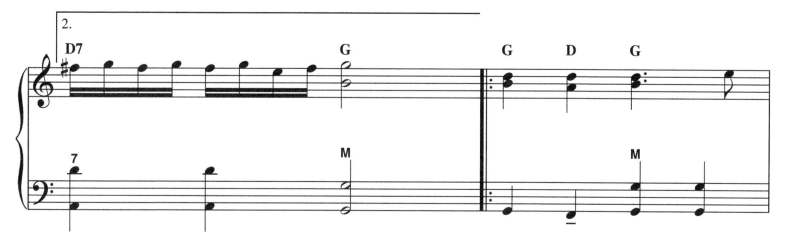

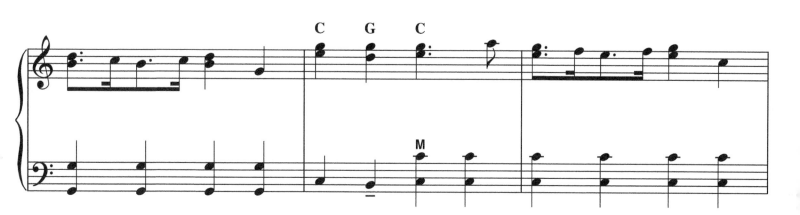

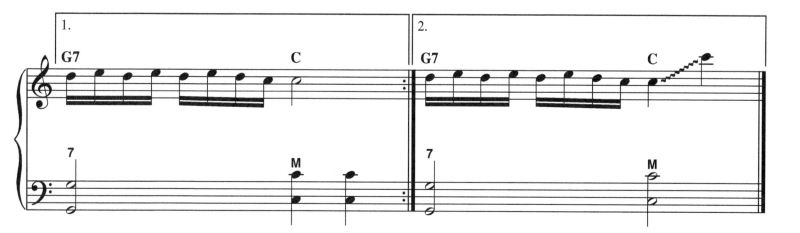

VALSE BLEUE

Words and Music by
ALFRED MARGIS

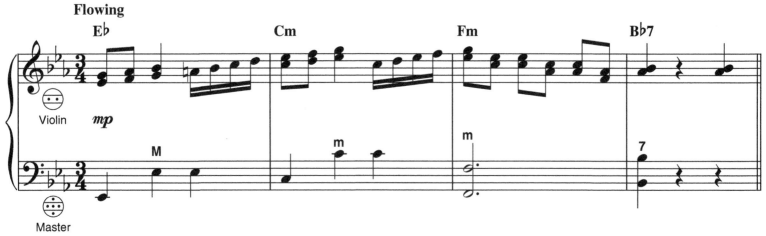

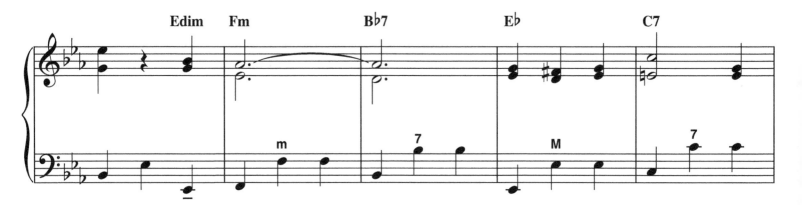

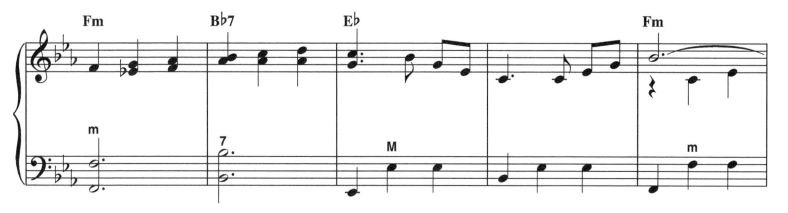

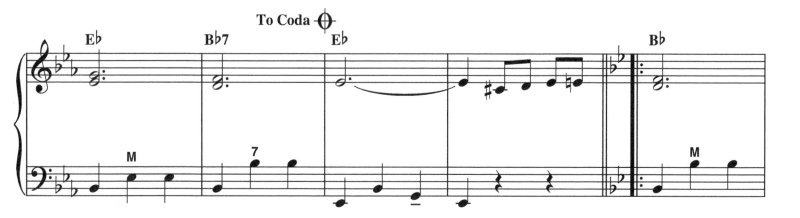